RADIANCE

RADIANCE

Experiencing Divine Presence

GINA LAKE

Endless Satsang Foundation

www.radicalhappiness.com

ISBN: 978-1475090123

CONTENTS

PREFACE

Many of you already realize your oneness with the Divine and All That Is. You already know that you are much vaster than who you think you are. It is possible to experience the mysterious truth about yourself by paying close attention to the many signs that reveal this great Mystery. The purpose of this book is to point out these clues so that you can more easily recognize yourself as the Divine—that which is creating and has created this *you* that you think you are and all that this *you* is experiencing. This book was given to me by my nonphysical teacher.

Gina Lake
January, 2006

CHAPTER 1

THE DIVINE IS EVERYWHERE

You Are Not Who You Think You Are

Who are you, really? Are you so-and-so with a certain past and a certain body and personality and certain roles talents, weaknesses, dreams, fears, and beliefs? You may define yourself to others in these ways, but that is not who you really are. Who you really are can only be discovered through deeper questioning and exploration and through a more subtle experiencing of that which is beyond all ideas about yourself. It can only be discovered when the mind is quiet and no longer telling you who you are. When all the ideas about yourself are stilled, then what remains is who you really are: Consciousness, Awareness, Stillness, Presence, Peace, Love, the Divine. You are that which is Nameless and yet has been given a thousand names.

To those of you who are not so sure about who you really are, you are not alone. Even those who have realized this are not always certain. The realization of who you are comes and goes to some extent depending on what you pay attention to. Even those who have realized the truth, that there is only one Being in all of existence, can temporarily forget who they really are when they become lost in believing their thoughts. The mind is very compelling, and giving your attention to it, will bring you back to the experience of yourself as separate from the rest of creation.

Nevertheless, you are not who you *think* you are. Thinking gives you the illusion of being someone, but you are not some-one but rather Oneness itself, the Divine masquerading as an individual. This masquerade is for the purpose of exploring this physical reality and for having the unique experiences you are having as some-one. The Divine is enjoying the experiences it is having through all of creation, even experiences you would consider unenjoyable. What the Divine enjoys is experience—

any experience. It created you just for that, or rather you created *you* just for that.

You may think you are not enjoying an experience, but if you touch deeply into yourself, you will discover enjoyment in even the most unpleasant experiences. The joy from these experiences comes simply from the ability to have them, the ability to be alive and experience them. The Divine is enjoying life and celebrating in every moment through every creation, regardless of what is being experienced. Therefore, it is possible for you to find joy in any experience as well when you align yourself with the divine Self in you, or *Essence*, instead of the personal self, or the *you* that you think you are.

This *you* is very difficult to please. It can be having a very nice experience and still not be happy. The *you* is programmed for unhappiness because it is programmed to seek that which can never bring true happiness. It goes after more and better and different from whatever is actually present, and that creates ceaseless searching and dissatisfaction with whatever is found. This is a very unhappy predicament, and yet this is the human condition.

This is why humans suffer, but you are not actually human, so it isn't necessary for you to suffer this way. Once you discover your true nature, it is possible for suffering to end, or at least be greatly diminished. The Divine doesn't suffer in its experience of life, and you don't have to either. You can experience the joy the Divine has in life in any moment if you turn your attention to the moment (where the Divine, as Essence, resides), but you have to want to and you have to make that choice. This is the greatest obstacle to happiness of all. Many experience the Truth that lies in the moment and turn away from it again and again because there is nothing in it for the *egoic mind*, which is the mind that is driven by the ego, or illusory personal self–the *you* that you think you are. The egoic mind is the familiar voice in your head, the ongoing mental commentary that accompanies whatever you do.

This *you* thinks of itself constantly. It is constantly forming thoughts about itself, which is how it creates itself. It describes itself to itself and to others, and that gives the *you* a sense of actually existing, when in fact, it exists only as a description. This description–this *you*–is made up of a jumble of ideas that are not even consistent, since they change from moment to moment, day to day. This *you* believes one thing one day and another thing the next. It likes something one day and the opposite the next. It sees itself one way one day and another way the next. And yet it seems so solid, so real, that this *you* is willing to argue with others over what it thinks, what it believes, and how it sees things. Where do all of these ideas come from?

They are just there. Stop a moment and look. The ideas that arise in your mind that define this *you* arise from nowhere and disappear into nowhere, only to be replaced by other ideas. They have no more reality or truth in terms of defining you than the last set of ideas or the next set of ideas. Ideas come and go, and they are as meaningless and random as what happens when you flip from station to station on the radio. It is just that certain ideas come and go more frequently on your particular radio station than on someone else's, but that doesn't make them any more real, true, or capable of defining who you are.

Who You Are

Who you are cannot be defined by words. Who you are lives in the space between words, in the Stillness that is ever-present and known only when the mental chatter has stopped or is no longer given attention. Who you are cannot be described; it can only be experienced. However, the experience of it is often missed because attention is being given to other things, particularly ideas. These ideas, when you are identified with the mind, seem more real and interesting than who you are because the mind is only interested in things it can understand, describe, and categorize.

Since there are plenty of things and ideas for the mind to get absorbed in, this *you* that is identified with the mind is very busy paying attention to things and to the thoughts that arise in the mind. When you are identified with the mind, you often give thoughts more attention even than things. This *you* that you think you are not only thinks itself into existence, but also everything else, in the sense that what it thinks affects how it perceives actual things and other aspects of reality. Thus, the mind filters and colors experience and gives experience its own spin.

The Divine intends it to be just this way. It created the mind to do exactly what it does. In order for the Divine to have a unique experience through every human being, it was necessary for every human being to have a separate sense of self and to forget the Oneness that is everyone's true nature. Thus, you have traded in the remembrance of your divinity for experiences. You learn and grow in love as a result of your experiences, and that is also intended by the Divine. It also intends that one day you will awaken to the truth of your divinity and express that in life, which will bring experience of a different kind as well as further evolution.

The goodness, or divinity, in you drives you forward in your evolution until you express that goodness increasingly in your actions and speech. The ego, which does not seek goodness and love, but pleasure and avoidance of pain, also drives your actions and creates experiences, many of which cause pain, but also evolution.

Eventually, you realize that love and goodness are what bring lasting happiness, and you find your way to living from the Heart, from Essence, more than from the egoic mind. When your identity shifts from the egoic mind to the Heart, where your divinity lies, you are said to have awakened to your true nature. It is the most significant point in your evolution because you are finally free of the domination of the egoic mind, and life is lived from a very different place.

Being Awake

Being awake doesn't mean you never identify with the egoic mind; it means you no longer believe the mind, even when you do find yourself identified with it. This may seem contradictory because identification with the mind usually entails believing it. When you are awake, however, the experience of identification is more like you know you are playing the role of someone who is believing the mind, while you know yourself as what is observing the entire drama. So although identification with the mind happens after awakening, identification doesn't last long, and it isn't a problem when it does. You know yourself as other than the self that is momentarily identified, and you spend most of your time in the experience of the moment.

After awakening, because you never lose sight of who you really are even when you are identified with the egoic mind, life feels very different. You can enjoy the play of consciousness as it moves in and out of identification. What does it matter what you are identified with once you know the truth? Consciousness enjoys playing the part it is playing in this lifetime. Once you awaken, it is really possible to enjoy this life, this character you are playing, and everything that happens to it because you know it is just a story that is being played out. That is why mystics and sages describe the world as a dream. From the perspective of someone who is awake, life feels very much like a dream in which you are aware that you are dreaming.

Such detachment allows you to enjoy life in a way that wasn't possible when you were attached to the outcome of the story you are living. When you are identified with the egoic mind, you have ideas about how you want the story of your life to go in all the presumably important areas: career, relationships, health, home, and family. You envision your life being a certain way, and you try to make it be that way. These thoughts are what the egoic mind, posing as the *you* that you think you are, is preoccupied with, and this can keep you very busy.

On the other hand, once you have awakened, you don't require life to be a certain way in order to be happy because you are already happy and you know that what you *thought* you needed to be happy isn't necessary for your happiness. You are happy because you are aligned with the divine Self that lives in and expresses itself through you: Essence. And, unlike other things of this world, Essence is eternal and eternally available and eternally fulfilling.

To know true happiness, all you have to do is choose to be aligned with Essence instead of the egoic mind. What the egoic mind chases after is often unattainable, and even when it is attained, it is never enough. The egoic mind always wants more, better, or different than whatever it already has. Its prescription for happiness leads only to unhappiness, discontentment, and suffering. Given this, choosing Essence over the ego would seem like such a clear choice. But there's a catch.

The Need to Choose

If it were easy to choose Essence over the ego, everyone would be happy and free from suffering. This choice is difficult because you are programmed to be attracted to thoughts and to the objects of the world. Without that programming, you would be born knowing your divinity, and you would miss out on the experience of feeling you are an independent entity with a will, and you would miss out on all the experiences, learning, and growth that go with that. This Mystery is designed to veil the truth of your divinity and the existence of only One so that that One can have experiences. It is through giving you a mind that is programmed in the way it is programmed that this is accomplished. So the catch is that you are programmed to choose the ego over Essence until a time comes in your evolution for the realization of the truth to surface.

Given that you are reading this now, it is likely that the time is approaching for this realization, if it hasn't already arrived. When the time comes to awaken, Essence calls to you in a number of ways, and you begin to experience Essence more often and for longer periods of time. What we will be exploring are some of the many ways the Divine calls to you and makes itself known. Some of these ways are so obvious that they are overlooked or discounted. Other ways require diligent looking before the Divine's face is seen.

The desire to experience the Divine and the choice to look for it come, of course, from the Divine itself, since there is no other. At a certain point in a person's evolution, the Divine seeks itself.

It calls to itself and awakens itself so that it can live and breathe more fully through that body, mind, and personality. It beckons itself Home. In the coming chapters, we are going to take a look at some of the ways the Divine does this. But first, it is important to realize that the Divine is everywhere and in everything, including within every experience.

Everywhere You Look

There is nowhere that the Divine is not. Stop a moment and really take this truth in, because the mind has a very different perception. If really grasped, this truth will change your life. Everything you see, everything and everyone that exists, and everything that happens is a manifestation of the Divine. The Divine is not only behind every good act, but also behind every evil one, which is what happens when the *you* that you think you are is lost in fear and the illusion of being separate. The Divine is both the perpetrator and the victim, the lover and the hater. It plays every role that has ever been played because there is no other. There is only the illusion of other.

Imagine that—there is no other! The mind is so good at imagining, but it has difficulty imagining Oneness because it goes against its programming. So when Oneness is experienced, as it is momentarily many times even in one day, it isn't acknowledged. Oneness goes unnoticed, unappreciated by the mind. Worse than that—Oneness is rejected by the egoic mind because acknowledging it would threaten its existence. The ego doesn't exist in Oneness; it can only exist in separateness. The ego is created by and perpetuates separation. That is the very definition of the ego. The ego and Oneness are at odds, or so it seems. However, Oneness designed life to be this way, so Oneness has no problem with the ego, although the ego has a problem with Oneness.

Everywhere it looks, the ego sees separation. It translates all the differences it sees as separation: The ego sees a tree, and because the tree is different from the ego's image of itself, the ego sees itself as separate from the tree. But is that true? Where did this definition of self come from, in which anything that is different from itself is seen as separate from itself?

It is the ego's own definition that creates the idea of separation: Different equals separation by the ego's own definition. The ego sees boundaries between things and people. It even creates boundaries conceptually through language and in terms of time and by holding certain beliefs. This is just how the egoic mind digests life. All these differences are seen by the ego as potentially dangerous and problematic. The ego is constantly on the defense, trying to protect itself from everything out there that is different from itself. Its world is full of fear, anxiety, jealousy, hatred, anger, and pain. This viewpoint and the sense of being separate is at the base of all suffering.

But reality is not as the ego supposes. There are no boundaries. There is no separate self in opposition to the world. There is only the Divine creating each moment fresh from itself. Everything is the Divine expressing itself as tree, as dog, as person, as thought, as emotion, as light, as sound. No boundaries. No one. Only One. Only the Divine creating and expressing itself through life.

CHAPTER 2

THE WINDOWS TO THE SOUL

Seeing Radiance

If the Divine had a face, it would be a radiant one. How do you know? Because its reflection on the physical plane is light and radiance and because that's what you see when the Divine, as Essence, looks out from your eyes. The world looks different when you are awake and aligned with Essence. It shines, it glows, it shimmers, it sparkles. People, plants, animals, and objects radiate the light of Being. They always have, but not everyone notices it. The ego doesn't. It's too busy comparing, judging, labeling, and evaluating what it sees to notice the radiance. When Essence looks out of your eyes, however, everything shimmers and shines.

This seeing is not like the usual seeing. It is subtler, but it is still experienced as seeing. It is as if the usual seeing becomes infused with light: The radiance of the Divine spills out of everything. It erases all boundaries and reveals that all is light. All is itself as light. All of creation shimmers as One Being.

Just as the objects in a painting belong to the painting rather than to themselves, the distinctions between objects are no longer seen as real, but as part of the design within a larger whole, which contains them. The painting would not be the same were anything left out. So it is with life: The differences create the Whole; they don't stand apart from it. Furthermore, as in a painting, everything in life is made from the same substance. It is all the Divine.

The mind sees boundaries between the objects in a painting. But by stepping back, the picture as a whole can be experienced, and that is what makes art powerful. Those who love art don't pick it apart and analyze it, but respond to it emotionally and spiritually. So it is with life: The mind picks it apart, and the Heart responds to it spiritually and emotionally (with love).

To see this radiance requires the lenses of perception to be purified, cleansed of the conditioning that perceives boundaries between objects and, moreover, cleansed of the mind's tendency to evaluate what it sees according to its conditioning. Eyes that are directed by the ego look for validation of the ego's viewpoint and threats to its safety and identity. The ego views the world and its contents, including people, from the standpoint of how something will affect its goals: Will it advance my goals or not? The ego is busy with its own inner mental world, not the real world. When it does see the real world, it is through the lens of desire: Will it get me what I want?

The process of healing your conditioning results in a gradual cleansing of the lenses of perception. You gradually come to see more radiance and less according to the ego's desires and goals. This coincides with greater happiness, peace, and contentment with life. The quieter the egoic mind becomes and the less dominant it is, the happier you become. This evolution takes place over many lifetimes. The endpoint is radiance itself: not only do you see radiance everywhere, but you also become radiant.

Being Radiant

As the lenses of perception become purified, the gateway to your soul is opened and the Divine begins to shine forth. It does this through the eyes. Once what comes into the eyes is no longer being filtered and distorted by the ego, the eyes become the means by which the Divine receives the world and, in turn, touches it.

The Divine receives the world and everything about the world with acceptance and without judgment. It loves the world. After all, the world is itself, and it has no reason to reject the world. The Divine loves creation for the possibilities it provides for experience. Through creation, the Divine has the opportunity to interact with itself, which as Oneness wasn't possible. What a great adventure and experiment this world is! Not even Oneness knows what its creations, who have lost touch with Oneness to some extent, will do.

This love for the world can be seen in the eyes of those who are in touch with Essence, and it is seen as radiance, love, peace, and joy. Those who see this in someone's eyes are attracted to it because love, peace, and joy are what everyone wants. All the seeking and striving on the part of the ego is an attempt to acquire love, peace, and joy—happiness. The ego just makes the mistake of looking for happiness in the wrong places. In fact, the egoic mind is the only thing in the way of happiness. It is the problem, not the solution. When the mind is quiet, all there is, is love, peace, and joy.

That truth is apparent in the eyes of those who are in touch with Essence. They convey this truth to others through their eyes. And looking into their eyes can cause others to drop into Essence and experience the same love, peace, contentment, and joy that is the nature of Essence. Wisdom, kindness, and good acts flow from Essence as well. Once the lenses of perception become clear, you become a conduit and catalyst for peace, love, and joy in the world.

The biggest clue to the mystery of who you really are is in the eyes. The Divine gives the secret away by appearing in the eyes. Nowhere else is the Divine more apparent than in the eyes of those who have already discovered the secret: There is only one Being here! When you look into another's eyes, you can feel your commonality with them, your Oneness. You don't have to be enlightened to have that experience, and either does the other person. Oneness shines through in the eyes of everyone.

Eyes can bring you Home if you allow them to. If you allow yourself to drop the thoughts that intervene between you and another for just a moment, then there You are, right there in the other's eyes! What a surprise. You experience this most often during sex and with others you love deeply, such as your children and pets because, with them, your defenses and judgments are diminished. Gazing into another's eyes while affirming your Oneness with them can help bring about the experience of Oneness.

Exercise: Seeing the Divine in Another

Take fifteen minutes or so to sit quietly with someone and look into one another's eyes. Get very comfortable and set aside all issues, concerns, judgments, and any other thoughts to just be present with this person. As you are looking into each other's eyes, just stay with that experience. If a thought comes up, notice it, and then go back to just looking. If your mind wanders, just bring your attention back to the eyes. When the mind isn't being identified with, Essence shines through the eyes. Notice this, without thinking about it or telling any stories about it. Notice the beauty of Essence in your partner. This is his or her true self. This is the Beloved. Beyond conditioning, all there is, is This.

Often, all that is needed to experience Essence is the willingness to. Essence is available in every moment. You just have to notice it and not turn away from it. You are much more willing to do this with people you already love, but it's possible to experience Essence and Essence's love with anyone if you choose to see the truth about him or her.

Even just one person who is doing this in a room full of people can change the atmosphere because Essence is contagious: Essence brings out Essence in others. If you align with Essence, you will become a catalyst for peace, love, and joy in the world. Have you noticed how contagious anger and negativity are? Fortunately, love is equally contagious and a much more rewarding experience.

Practice cultivating loving interactions with others by choosing to see their divine nature, no matter what they are doing or saying or how they look, and you will not only live in peace and joy, but also bring others to peace and joy. Just by noticing the Divine in their eyes, this transformation in you and in others can take place.

Transformation really is this simple, but the ego will come up with all sorts of reasons to discount what it sees in someone's eyes and avoid looking for the Divine there or anywhere else. The ego doesn't believe the Divine exists. It asks: Where is the proof? The ego is afraid of what it sees in the eyes of others. It doesn't know what to think of this. It has no words or explanations for what it sees because that doesn't fit into the ego's paradigm or even into most religious belief systems. The ego doesn't believe there is a Mystery here because the Mystery is not something that can be quantified. All it knows is what it wants, and that becomes the reason for doing and saying what it does.

Moving from the Ego to Essence

Everyone experiences Essence several times a day, but the experience is often so brief that it doesn't affect the egoic state of consciousness that most live their lives in. When Essence is experienced for longer periods of time, it can shift you from ego identification to Essence, which is your natural state.

The more you experience Essence, the easier it is to choose it, so you naturally move, over the course of many lifetimes, from ego identification to Essence because Essence is a much more pleasant state. To live more continually aligned with Essence, the habit of ego identification needs to be broken, which isn't so easy.

Because you are programmed to pay attention to the egoic mind and believe what it tells you about yourself, others, and life, most people's lives unfold according to the ego's ideas, desires, and demands— their conditioning. The problem is that happiness can't be found in following the false beliefs and values of the ego. Unhappiness is the certain result of allowing the egoic mind to run your life.

Essence sees life more truly. When you are identified with Essence, you see life more as it really is, without the filter of your conditioning. From Essence, life is interesting, challenging, fun, beautiful, touching, and rich. Experiences aren't categorized, judged, or labeled as good or bad. They just *are*, in all of their richness and complexity, because in truth, a thousand stories could be told about any experience, and those stories would still not reflect the whole experience. The ego attempts to define experience in words, according to its conditioning, which divorces you from the complexity and reality of the experience. It turns experience into ideas, which sap the life out of life. Living from the mind is like eating a picture of food instead of the real thing. No wonder so many people feel empty and unfulfilled. Only reality truly satisfies.

Seeing from Essence's Eyes

Seeing from Essence's eyes is a lot like how very young children see. They don't have the degree of conditioning, facts, and concepts yet that older children and adults have, which filter and color experience. The interchange between young children and their environment is much purer. When you are aligned with Essence instead of the ego, conditioning still exists, but it doesn't interfere with experience as it used to. Your thoughts are recognized for what they are: conditioning that is mostly untrue and not helpful.

For the most part, your conditioning takes you down the path to unhappiness, not happiness. So unhappiness and the desire to be truly happy ultimately drive the choice to become aligned with

Essence. What stands between you and happiness is essentially just a choice, the choice to be aligned with Essence instead of the ego by saying yes to Essence's perceptions instead of the ego's. Here is an exercise that will help you see from Essence's eyes:

Exercise: Seeing from Essence's Eyes

Look at something in your environment and notice how quickly the mind comes in with a judgment, analysis, or some other comment about what you are looking at. Move your gaze from one object to another and just look and notice what the mind does. As long as you continue to just look without thinking about the object you are looking at, you will see as Essence sees. But the moment you begin to think, you lose contact with the object and with the moment, and you become identified with the ego and its perceptions. Essence doesn't evaluate as it looks; it experiences without evaluation. This looking is joyful and uncomplicated by the negativity of the mind. What a relief it is to be Home! This way of looking can become your ordinary way of seeing and being.

Essence perceives life as a whole and as essentially good. It accepts and loves everything simply because it exists. Essence doesn't demand that life be any way other than the way it is. When you are accepting and loving toward life and your experience, you are experiencing Essence and its love, peace, contentment, joy, and acceptance.

If you stay in acceptance long enough, you will begin to notice the radiance that accompanies the love, peace, and joy you are experiencing. There is a visual accompaniment to being aligned with Essence, which gives objects a shimmery glow and subtle fluidity. Objects are experienced more as flowing into each other rather than having distinct boundaries. The more you pay attention to this subtle visual experience, the longer it lasts and the deeper it becomes. Usually, it's only noticed briefly, but it actually never disappears. Whenever you turn your attention to it, there it is. You can train yourself to see this way more continually, and once your identity shifts more permanently to Essence, that is the experience.

Seeing in this way produces a softness in your eyes and demeanor because Essence's relationship to life is nonviolent and peaceful. Essence takes action when action is called for, but it doesn't try to force or manipulate life to conform to ideas, as the ego does, because Essence is free of ideas about the way things should be. To Essence, the way things are is exactly how they should be.

Essence may have intentions for the next moment, but it doesn't try to change the current one. Essence does influence and shape life, but during it, not after the fact. It flows with life and shapes life while life is moving where it is moving. This is very different from the ego, which opposes whatever is showing up and tries to change what already is.

Those who are strongly identified with the ego often have a hardness and dullness in their eyes, which reflects their determination of will and lack of contact with reality. Nevertheless, Essence shines in those eyes too, behind that hardness and dullness. It flickers in and out, depending on how intensely they are involved with ideas about how things should be. When they are more quiet mentally and relaxed physically, Essence is there in their eyes. Essence is behind everyone's eyes, but it is covered over when mental activity is very strong. You can actually see people thinking.

When you are aligned with Essence, it becomes apparent that Essence is behind your eyes, not only to others, but also to yourself because you feel Essence there. Essence is felt as Consciousness, or Awareness, looking out through your eyes. That Awareness feels like who you are, and your body feels like just a vehicle for moving in the world. Although Awareness isn't limited to the head and eyes, it's often strongly felt in that area because Awareness tends to become localized there.

When you are aligned with Essence, you know yourself as that localized point of Consciousness that is connected to your particular body, mind, and personality. It's clear that the body, mind, and personality are not who you are, but only something that makes it possible for Essence to function in the world. This detachment from the body, mind, and personality makes it possible to see the connectedness and perfection of all of life. It makes it possible to truly love.

When you are aligned with Essence, your eyes have a look to them that is recognizable as Essence but difficult to describe. They have a depth, intensity, and fire about them and a piercing, yet gentle, and infinite quality. An actual energy is transmitted from this gaze, from Essence through the eyes, that can bring others into alignment with

Essence to the extent that they are willing to have that experience. This is well known in spiritual circles headed by spiritual masters or gurus. Photos have the same capacity for transmission, even ones of deceased spiritual masters.

In part, this transmission is made possible by the desire and openness of the recipient, who puts himself or herself in a position of receiving by being in the presence of a spiritual master or guru. Doing this is an affirmation of the willingness to experience Essence, and this prayer is always answered, at least to some extent.

The eyes are one of the ways the Divine brings itself Home. They are its calling cards. The eyes indicate the existence of the Divine as well as transmit a frequency that causes those who are ready and open to resonate with their divine nature. The eyes not only provide a visual experience of the Divine, but also have the ability to shift your consciousness.

Those who have experienced the eyes' ability to shift consciousness know the truth on a deep level and need no more convincing, while those who haven't have difficulty believing what they haven't experienced, and understandably so. And yet the

Divine is not only experienced through the eyes, but also in many other ways in the world, if only the ego would notice and open to those revelations.

CHAPTER 3

LOVE IS EVERYWHERE

Love Is Your Nature

You can tell that love is your nature because love is what you experience when you are still and your mind is quiet. Then the Heart naturally opens, and it expresses itself as love. This love is not romantic love, but more like acceptance, joy, gratitude, and contentment with life. It's subtler, softer, gentler, and less personal than romantic love, which has a giddiness and an excitement about it. With romantic love, you expect the world; with this love, you know yourself as the world. With romantic love, your focus is on the other; with this love, you know yourself as the other. With romantic love, there are two; with this love, there is only One.

Your natural state is a state of love, acceptance, peace, contentment, and quietude. Gone is the need to get, keep, improve, and think. In this Stillness, there's little desire for thought or anything else. When you experience love, acceptance, peace, and contentment, it means you have dropped into Essence and are no longer identified with the egoic mind, which can be recognized by the opposite qualities: a lack of love, acceptance, peacefulness, and contentment.

At your core, you are love, acceptance, peace, and contentment. These same qualities are at everyone's core, although they are often obscured by identification with the egoic mind. Ego identification is the usual state of consciousness, but not the natural state of consciousness. The natural state of consciousness is love, and you are here to discover that. Your programming, which gives you the impression that you are the ego and the mind, conceals this truth.

Love is the glue that holds the universe together. This is an esoteric statement that can't be understood by the mind. You have to take this truth on faith. Once you do, you begin to see love everywhere. Your beliefs have a powerful impact on your experience of life. They filter your perceptions. For example, if you believe that love is everywhere, which it is, then you'll experience that. If, on the other hand, you believe that evil is everywhere, that is what you'll see, no matter how much love is in front of your eyes.

It's important to acknowledge that love is everywhere because doing that counteracts the ego's assumption that love isn't everywhere and that life isn't safe and supportive. The importance of counteracting the ego's negative beliefs is that, unless you do, you are likely to remain identified with the ego. To wake up to your divine nature and live in alignment with that instead of the ego, you have to train yourself to see life as Essence sees it instead of as the ego sees it. The more you do this, the more Essence will begin to live through you, and you will express Essence in the world instead of the ego. The reward for this is true happiness and peace and the capacity to bring others to true happiness and peace.

Every Act Is an Act of Love

Mother Theresa is remembered and revered for her great service to humanity and her ability to see the

Divine in everyone. When people think of love and the service that naturally flows from love, she often comes to mind. However, love has many other faces. It is visible in the simplest gestures and acts performed by very ordinary people living very ordinary lives: Love pushes a child on a swing, love drives safely, love shops for food, love listens, love greets, love waves, love touches, love smiles, love laughs, love kisses, love sings, love plays, and loves creates.

Exercise: Noticing Love

Notice all the ways you express love in your life. Notice the ways others express love. Love is everywhere, quietly and simply behind the scenes, being expressed in every moment. The ego's world is absent of love, and when you are identified with it, you see only problems and lack. The ego overlooks the evidence that love is behind and driving all life. Love is the juice that fuels life. You love to move, to breathe, to be alive. You even love to fight and have problems. Essence loves it all, even the chaos, messiness, and challenges. No matter what is happening, it is possible to experience Essence loving it. Love is really the only constant in the universe.

In fact, everything that people do is an act of love. Even those who choose to steal from or harm others are doing so out of love for themselves because they believe they need to do that to be safe or happy. Not all acts appear loving, but at their core, those who do them have the intention to do good at least for themselves, although possibly at the expense of others.

Harmful acts are attempts, although misguided ones, on the part of those who do them to preserve their own life or get something they feel they need to be happy. As you evolve, you become concerned about preserving the lives of those you love in addition to yourself. This circle eventually widens to include all of humanity, perhaps even at the expense of your own life.

If you were able to see love in every action, there would be no cause for judgment, which only leads to more separation, hatred, retribution, and suffering in the world. Dropping all judgments doesn't mean you would allow evil and not stand up for justice. Rather, it means you wouldn't be contributing to the separation and hatred that support and feed the sense the ego has that it must oppose others to keep itself safe.

When egos receive love and compassion, they resonate with it and express love, perhaps not immediately if there's a great deal of wounding, but eventually. Love heals, and it helps you evolve out of the fear that is part of ego identification into the peace of Essence. On the other hand, judgment, hatred, and retribution separate you, which confirms the ego's suspicion that it needs to do everything in its power to protect itself and get what it wants from a hostile world. This negative attitude is contagious, and it creates a very unpleasant world. You can do your part in turning this negativity around by seeing love in every act and remembering that every human being is inherently good.

Affirming someone's inherent goodness allows you to feel compassion for the suffering that person is creating, for himself or herself and everyone else involved, out of ignorance of the truth. As a result, you become more interested in dispelling ignorance and healing those involved than judging or punishing the wrongdoer. The human condition is such that you are not able to choose well because you don't understand who you really are and what is needed to find true happiness. You make choices that bring suffering to yourself and others. But this is all part of your spiritual evolution. No one ever became enlightened who wasn't first lost in the illusion of separation and hurting himself or herself and others. Everyone passes through this stage in evolution, and the responsibility falls on those who've already passed this way to help those who lack understanding.

Love Is All Around

As difficult as it may be to see love in certain acts and to see the goodness in certain people, it isn't difficult to find loving acts and loving people in this world. Love shines through in everyone to one degree or another because it can't be hidden or suppressed. Some have discovered the joy of loving acts and practice love consciously. Although most people may not be operating at this level, most do try to be loving to others, especially those close to them. In nearly every interaction, you see people making an effort to be loving. Politeness, smiles, consideration, helpfulness, receptivity, and attention are all ways people show their love and good will. Just because those expressions aren't always pure doesn't diminish the fact that love is driving them.

Although the ego is motivated to get its needs met and most people are identified with it, the Divine is alive and well within everyone and inspiring every person to express love. What interferes with expressing love is the tendency to be absorbed in your mind and thoughts about yourself and what you want and need rather than about how you might express love.

You can train yourself to counteract the ego's tendencies. When you decide to dedicate yourself to expressing love, you choose in each new moment to express love instead of following the egoic mind. Very few people are this committed to love, but that is where spiritual evolution is taking you. It is taking you toward expressing love in every moment.

Attention

Giving attention is a very basic form of love, which can be seen everywhere, and a way that love can be expressed very simply in the world. What you give your attention to is what you love. If you are giving your attention to the egoic mind, you are loving it and joining with it. If you are giving your attention to others, you are loving them and joining with them. Asking yourself, "What am I giving my attention to?" can be an excellent spiritual practice, and it will help you break the habit of identifying with the egoic mind.

Giving your attention to others is often at odds with giving your attention to your mind because the mind isn't interested in others. It's only interested in itself, its thoughts, its opinions, and its perceptions. To give your attention to others is a gift of love, because to do this, you must override the ego's tendency to give attention to itself and its needs. It takes some effort to overcome the programming to be self-focused and to become more other-focused. When you give your attention to others, you are expressing love in a most basic and simple way.

Giving attention to someone can be a powerful force for good. When you give attention to others, you are channeling love energy to them, regardless of how you might feel about them from the level of your personality. The choice to give attention to others is a loving choice. It connects them with the love energy that is their true nature and yours, and that's a gift. This all happens on very subtle levels, but it's still felt by people, who welcome attention and are often deeply touched by someone paying attention to them. Giving others attention is a way of acknowledging your Oneness with them and catalyzing the experience of Oneness in them, however subtle that experience might be.

Giving others attention causes them to feel love, and that comes back to you and goes out to others as well, so giving your attention to others is ultimately much more rewarding than giving your attention to the mind. Everyone wants love more than anything else because being in touch with your true nature is satisfying, unlike many of the other things the ego tries to attain that bring only fleeting satisfaction. As a result, giving attention to others becomes easier the more it is practiced.

Giving attention is equally rewarding when you give it to whatever you are doing. The ego draws you into its unreal world of thought. It entices you to pay attention to the mind with juicy thoughts about the past, fantasies about the future, and thoughts that build up the ego and sense of being special, which often involve tearing other people down. Giving your attention, instead, to whatever is going on in the moment is an act of loving life rather than rejecting the moment by escaping into the ego's mental world.

Whenever you give your attention to what is actually going on in the present moment, you are rewarded by experiencing love, peace, and contentment. Giving attention to real life instead of to the mind aligns you with love. However, you are programmed to move away from the moment. To counteract thiat programming, you have to learn to give your attention to what is real, to what is showing up *now*. When you do that, you become free of the egoic mind's ceaseless discontentment, negativity, and judgment. All you have ever had to do to be free of suffering is turn your attention away from the mind, away from what is not real, and onto the present moment.

The present moment is where your true nature and the qualities of your true nature can be experienced. Only when you are in the moment fully can you experience real love, acceptance, contentment, peace, and joy. All you have to do to experience those qualities is put your attention on what is happening *now* instead of on your thoughts.

Acceptance

One of the reasons you turn away from the moment is that you are programmed to reject life as it is. You want life on your own terms, but it can never be that way. Even if the ego could have life on its own terms, which the ego does experience briefly and occasionally, it would soon want more or different or better than that. The ego doesn't accept life, which is one reason the ego doesn't want to give it attention.

The ego would rather give attention to its fantasies, dreams, memories, opinions, judgments, and even fears than to the actual reality of any moment, which in addition to being imperfect (from the ego's point of view), is impossible to control or predict. The unpredictability of life and the ego's lack of control of it are deeply disturbing to the ego. Touching into reality makes the ego very uncomfortable because it is faced with the truth that it's not the one making life happen. As long as the ego remains in its made-up reality, it can play at being king. It pretends that it can make life go its way. It denies the obvious reality and chooses to believe what it wants to about reality.

Accepting whatever is happening drops you into Essence and into a state of happiness, peace, and contentment. That state is immediately uncomfortable for the ego, so the experience of happiness and peace doesn't usually last long. The ego finds fault even with peace, declaring it boring, and drums up a problem to think about and solve. If you agree with the ego's assessment of the moment, you are back in identification with it instead of with Essence. Fortunately, acceptance can bring you right back into the moment. Once you are aware of the power of acceptance to drop you into Essence, you can use acceptance more consciously to do that.

Acceptance is synonymous with love. Love accepts. You could say that acceptance is the definition of love. So when you accept what is happening, you land in love's territory. However, to stay there, you have to keep accepting what's happening, and that can be challenging because the mind comes into nearly every moment with a reason to leave it. You must say no to the mind again and again before its hold is loosened. The more you say no to the mind, the weaker it gets, and the more you say yes to it, the stronger it gets.

Detaching from the mind takes diligence, commitment, and choice, and you are the only one who can make that commitment and choice. To some extent, your spiritual evolution is in your hands. Other factors determine how and when you will unfold spiritually, but how fast you advance is largely up to you and your choices.

Accepting what is happening isn't as difficult as you may think. You only have to accept what is happening in the present moment, not in every moment throughout time. The ego has difficulty accepting what's happening because it spins a negative story about what it means for future moments. For instance, if you are feeling sick, the ego causes you to suffer over it by telling you how awful being sick is and what a negative impact it will have on your life. The stories it spins are all lies. It never predicts the future accurately.

Accepting what's happening is also not as difficult as you may think because accepting it doesn't mean you have to like it. All you have to do is accept that you don't like what's happening, if that is the case. Accepting what's happening just means you are willing to let it be the way it is. After all, what other choice do you have, since it is the way it is?

The only other choice is to argue with what's happening, complain about it, try to ignore it, or try to change it, which is what the ego does in nearly every moment. This is a recipe for suffering and doesn't change what is happening; it only makes what's happening unpleasant. By allowing whatever is happening to be happening, you align yourself with life instead of opposing it, and that makes every moment, regardless of what is happening, peaceful.

When the moment is okay just the way it is and your energy is not taken up in opposing it, you can really be present to whatever is happening. What you discover is that every moment has much more to it than what you like or don't like about it. Every moment is rich with complexity, dimension, and beauty. The ego paints the moment as black or white, good or bad. It has a simplistic view of what is happening according to its likes and dislikes, but the moment is not simple in the least. It's interestingly changeable, unpredictable, and intelligent. Who knows what will happen next? You never know. From the perspective of Essence, life's unpredictability is delicious, exciting, and fascinating. When you are in acceptance, you feel that way too about life.

When you are accepting, you are expressing Essence. And when you are accepted by others, you are experiencing Essence. Think of all the times in one day you are either accepting or experiencing acceptance from others. Every time acceptance happens, Essence is showing up in your life. Love is everywhere in the form of acceptance: You accept the sky, you accept gravity, you accept your breathing, you accept the color of the trees, you accept the silence between sounds, you accept the space between objects. You accept the majority of what is. This is You loving life and allowing it to be the way that it is.

The mind interrupts this peace, this love, by telling you that something is not right, not good, not desirable: "That dog shouldn't be barking." "The sun shouldn't be so hot." "It shouldn't be so windy." If you agree with the mind, you suffer. If you don't, you stay in Essence, in allowing whatever is to be the way it is.

The egoic mind will tell you that accepting life means you won't ever do anything. It tries to scare you out of accepting by making acceptance equal to passivity, laziness, and a lack of discrimination, which the ego deems dangerous to survival.

Acceptance is dangerous to the ego's survival, but it's not dangerous to your survival. Acceptance is a more effective strategy for survival than anything the ego has to offer. Acceptance is love, and love connects you with everything because it connects you with who you really are, which is everything. What could be more beneficial to survival than being connected to everything and knowing you are everything? Is there any reason that You, as the Divine, would not take care of you, as the creation? You are being taken care of and so is everyone else. The ego not only can't take credit for your survival, but it has interfered with it more than it has helped.

Something else besides the ego is living your life, and the more you allow it to do that, the more it will take over. Essence has been living through you and expressing itself through you as much as you have allowed it to. Every person is an expression of Essence to a greater or lesser degree. The Divine is moving, speaking, doing, creating, laughing, playing, and working through each of you to the extent that you allow it to, but it is there in everyone. If you want to have an experience of the Divine, you are having it! And so is everyone else.

You are not separate from the Divine. The ego is the sense that you are a separate person apart from the Divine, but that is just an idea. The ego is just the idea, "I exist as a separate entity." It isn't true. You are the Divine in disguise as a human being. The more you come to see that you are not who you think you are, the more you will experience who you really are and who everyone else really is. The Divine is everywhere.

CHAPTER 4

THE DIVINE IN ACTION

The Divine Lives Through You

The ego is not the only thing moving this body of yours. Many times in one day, the Divine moves you to take action and speak, while you are under the impression that *you* are doing these things. You are programmed to feel that you are separate, and part of this programming is the sense that *you* are doing what you are doing rather than being moved by an Intelligence greater than this *you*.

Many of you do have a sense that you are being moved through life, which being aligned with Essence feels like. The more you are aligned with Essence, the more you feel this. However, most people are identified with the ego most of the time, and for them, the sense of being moved by something beyond them is more rare and fleeting. Nevertheless they feel it too, if only occasionally. When it is felt, it is very rewarding. Moving through life with so little resistance feels good. It's a welcome relief from the usual struggle inherent in ego identification.

When action or speech is inspired by Essence, it flows spontaneously and easily. You feel compelled to do or say something without thinking about it ahead of time. You don't question it; you just do it. Your action or speech feels effortless, natural, and authentic—without ego. It feels like it isn't *you* doing or speaking, but more like it is coming through you, and you are just the vehicle for it. The result feels good, clean, and right.

Everyone has had this experience, but not everyone acknowledges it as the Divine, or Essence, moving through them. The more it is recognized, the more it will happen. The Divine expresses itself through you only as much as you allow it to. Those who recognize divine Presence are more likely to express it. Those who don't recognize it tend to find this experience unsettling. They distrust it because they don't understand it, and are therefore likely to interfere with it in the future. Gradually, the Divine makes itself known in every life, and it patiently waits for you to be ready to express it more fully in your life.

Meanwhile, the Divine does whatever it can to influence your choices. Since the egoic mind is the prominent voice for most people, the Divine has to find a way to circumvent it or work with it. So that is what the Divine does: It works within the life the ego is trying to create. Essence speaks to you mostly through your intuition and by nudging you toward action. What you choose to do is based on listening to either the egoic mind or your intuition and these nudges. These two different voices, or impetuses toward action and speech, coexist. You get to choose which one you will respond to.

Most people are used to responding to their thoughts rather than their intuition, so the ego often ends up shaping decisions more than Essence. As you evolve, this shifts, and the egoic mind becomes less prominent, and Essence becomes more prominent. This shift happens in part because you discover that following the egoic mind doesn't bring real happiness and fulfillment, while following the intuition (when it is accurately followed) does.

As you evolve, you become better at interpreting your intuition, since intuition is developed through experience. Through trial and error, you learn how to decipher Essence's communication. Eventually, you will become so good at it that you will only depend on the mind for the practical things the mind was designed for, such as reading maps or following directions.

Seeing the Divine in Your Actions

What moves your hands? What breathes your body? What laughs? What wakes up? What jumps out of bed in the morning? These kinds of actions are mostly spontaneous. For the most part, you don't decide to do these things; they just happen. A lot just happens. Think about it. Notice how many of the things you do just happen without having given them a thought beforehand. Many of the things you do without thinking are inspired by Essence. Some of your automatic reactions and responses are conditioning, but just notice all the times they aren't. Where do these spontaneous actions arise from? Why do you get out of bed one moment and not another? Why do you pick up the phone to call someone one moment and not another? What determines when you do these things?

The Divine has more to do with the timing of your actions than you might realize. You know you will get out of bed sometime, because that's what people do in the morning, but why in that second? Maybe the mind made a decision, and you complied with that. But if getting up just happened without making a decision, who chose to get up then? The mind chooses much of the time, but begin to notice all the times the mind doesn't choose, and action is still taken and words are spoken. When you look, you will see that there is a very great mystery here, and that mystery points to who you really are.

There is something else living this life that has been masquerading as the *you* that you think you are. This *you* is just a thought, while this something else is real, but it isn't a being or a thing, and it is not separate from anything else. It cannot be touched, seen, or defined because any definition could not contain the whole truth. It is too vast and mysterious to comprehend, and you aren't meant to. Your mind cannot comprehend this Mystery, and that is what keeps it a mystery.

However, as with any great mystery, there are clues that point to it. One of these clues lies in the mystery of who chooses to act or speak. It is clear enough when the mind chooses to act or speak because thoughts precede that choice. But what about all the times when you act or speak without thought or conditioning driving those actions or speech? If you pay close attention, you will discover that you act or speak spontaneously more often than as a result of some thought you had.

These spontaneous actions and speech can tell you a lot about your true nature and what this Mystery intends for your life. You will notice that these spontaneous actions and speech never harm anyone, but rather support and enhance life. You will notice that love, kindness, gentleness, joy, and truth are expressed by this Mystery that is the real you. You will notice that it loves life and doesn't resist jumping into it and taking action when that is needed. It speaks when speaking is called for, and it speaks with wisdom. When words are not necessary, it is silent. When action is not necessary, it rests. The Divine expresses itself even in the absence of action and speech. Sometimes it just rests in whatever else is happening without intervening. It moves in and out of interaction with life: Sometimes it acts, and sometimes it is still. But it is always present.

This Presence can be felt, whether it is actually moving through you, moving through someone else, or just resting quietly. It is felt as energy, consciousness, or awareness, as if someone is present and looking on, either out through your eyes or someone else's, or presiding over life from a distance. For many, this Presence is subtle; for others, it is felt strongly. As you become more aware of it and acknowledge it, the experience of Presence strengthens. Eventually, your sense of self becomes identified with Presence instead of the ego. You come to know yourself as Presence, Essence, rather than the *you* that you think of yourself as.

Until you come to see yourself as Presence and identify with that, you experience Presence as something outside yourself, as if God is watching over you. This stage naturally precedes the discovery of yourself as Presence. This stage acts as a bridge between identification with the ego and identification with Essence. During this stage, the goodness of Essence is attributed to something outside yourself, to God, rather than to yourself. The ego is more comfortable with this attribution because it gets to remain dominant. You still get to be someone with problems that need to be solved by the ego. Once you awaken and your identity shifts from the ego to Essence, the ego loses its sense of reality and its power. It doesn't disappear, but it is no longer the dominant influence and the central player.

Seeing the Divine in the Actions of Others

The Divine is equally apparent in the actions of others, especially when that person is strongly aligned with Essence. When that happens, that person acts as a conduit for Essence, bringing those around him or her into alignment as well. Actions from Essence are not only satisfying and fulfilling, but also powerful. They have the power to draw others into Essence, and for those who aren't used to experiencing Essence, it is a profound experience.

You can recognize Essence in action in others by how you feel around them. You feel uplifted, positive, happy, and strong. Life feels good and right, and what they are doing or saying feels good and right. You may feel moved or touched by something they said. You may even feel chills or tingles, which seem to confirm your feelings about what they said. These kinds of actions and communications happen more frequently than you may realize. Once you become more aware of them, you see they happen all the time.

The Divine works through you and through others to make the world go around. Through others, it brings you information, insight, comfort, help, truth, wisdom, healing, support, and whatever else you need to evolve as you are meant to. You do the same for others. The Divine uses you to express and accomplish what it intends to, and it uses others the same way. You don't have to be enlightened to be used this way; you only have to be alive.

You have always been a vehicle for the Divine to some degree, mostly without being aware of it. Once you become aware of this phenomenon, you can ask to serve more in this way, and it will happen more consciously. There is no limit to what can be accomplished when the ego is set aside and you are aligned with that which moves all of creation.

Through each of you, the Divine works uniquely and distinctly. Everyone has certain talents and strengths that are being developed and expressed in this lifetime. The Divine has a plan for you for this lifetime, and that plan is unique to you. The Divine works through every person differently, depending on his or her skills and talents. It will use you in the ways it intends, and that is what will most fulfill you.

Some plans have very simple goals, such as learning to be a better mother or developing musical talent, while others have more grand goals, such as helping to solve the population problem or discovering a cure for a disease. Whatever your plan is, it will be conveyed to you through your intuition and through drives, inspiration, and urges to take certain actions. Essence guides you to fulfill its plan by causing you to be attracted to certain activities and not to others. You will feel drawn to learning or doing whatever you need to fulfill your plan.

The ego can interfere with this plan either by sidetracking you with its goals or through judgments or other disparaging remarks that may block you from moving in the direction that would be most fulfilling. Other people may block you as well. Those who are strongly identified with the ego, may tell you what you should and shouldn't do, as if they know, because that is how the ego interacts with others.

The ego assumes a position of rightness, and it tries to impose its views on others. It doesn't experience or trust any other force in the universe but itself. Although the egoic mind is ill-equipped to give advice about life, it assumes that it is and that doing that is its job. Believing the mind leads many astray for a time, until Essence is once again able to bring its influence to bear. Essence nearly always prevails, at least to some extent. Very few are totally lost to the dictates of the egoic mind—fortunately.

The way you can tell if your actions are aligned with the ego or Essence is how you feel. Do you feel happy, hopeful, excited, and enlivened when you think about or pursue a certain direction? That is Essence saying yes to that. If you feel confused, unsure, negative, fearful, and unexcited about a direction, then that direction is probably not right for you, or at least not at this time. Is your ego or someone else's telling you that you *should* do that? Following *shoulds* won't bring you happiness, while following the deeper drives of Essence will.

The ego generates desires to move you, while Essence generates drives. The ego's desires and Essence's drives are very different. They are experienced differently, and they bring different results. When you follow the ego's desires, you learn, grow, and evolve as a result of the circumstances you create. You won't find much lasting happiness in fulfilling those desires, but you may get some satisfaction from learning something from pursuing those goals. The Divine seeks experience, learning, and growth through you, so it allows you to follow the ego's desires. The ego leads you to believe, however, that fulfilling its desires is the route to happiness, which it isn't.

Essence, on the other hand, produces drives to pursue certain goals and do certain things. Following these drives and accomplishing these goals brings deep fulfillment. Happiness is a byproduct because, in aligning yourself with Essence's goals, you also become aligned with Essence's qualities, and happiness is one of these qualities. If you want a happy and fulfilled life, align your actions with Essence's intentions for you. This is not as hard as it might sound. Just listen to your intuition and Essence's nudges instead of the ego's fears and *shoulds* and *should nots*. Listen to your intuition instead of your mind.

Aligning Your Actions with Essence

Thinking is what most stands in the way of knowing what actions Essence would have you take. This is true for two reasons: 1) You are programmed to believe that thinking has the answers to how to live your life, so you look to the mind for them, and 2) When you are busy thinking, you don't notice the intuition and nudges that come from Essence. Nevertheless, it's easy enough to tell when your actions are being driven by the ego and when they are being driven by Essence.

When Essence is driving your actions, those actions are fueled by a deep sense of dedication, regardless of how things might turn out. That dedication is marked by a willingness to live in the unknown, take risks, and make sacrifices. Those actions are driven more by passion than willfulness, and action is taken for the joy of it and less for the possible reward. There is a sense of needing to do something, which at times can seem irrational. The ego, on the other hand, is very rational about what it pursues, often pursuing things solely for the dream of a particular reward. Its actions are driven by wanting the things it values: power, money, safety, material things, security, comfort, pleasure, recognition, and success.

There is also a difference in how Essence and the ego pursue things. While Essence moves with the flow of life, taking advantage of opportunities that present themselves, the ego pushes and tries to make things happen according to its ideas and in keeping with a particular timetable. The ego makes a plan and tries to implement it. When you are aligned with Essence, on the other hand, you uncover Essence's plan and follow it as it naturally unfolds. *You* don't make the plan, but rather tune into the plan that already exists. These are two very different ways of living, and they bring very different experiences. Living in alignment with Essence brings much more happiness—and ease.

When you are aligned with Essence, action comes about naturally, organically (out of the moment and circumstances), easily, and clearly. When action comes from Essence, it is clear, positive, and usually carried out with ease. Things fall into place. When action comes from the ego, on the other hand, it is often confused and uncertain, although willful. It may run into unforeseen problems and roadblocks. The ego tends to disregard the current reality and focus on the desired outcome, sometimes to the exclusion of important facts. The ego sees what it wants to see and makes choices based on that, so its choices are often not wise or well timed.

To discover Essence's plan, you have to pay attention to what is coming out of the moment because the plan is unfolding in every moment. You can't go to a book and read about it. You can't figure it out by thinking about it. You can only discover it by paying attention to the present moment. What is happening? What inspiration, urges, and drives are coming out of the moment? What do you feel moved to do now? What *are* you doing now?

You are never done asking these questions because each moment is new and different. To find out what to do next, you have to keep looking into the present moment. However, it is best not to look into it with your mind. Just notice what the *experience* is. What is moving? What are you experiencing? What intuitions or ideas give you joy when they arise? Those are the ones to follow. Where is your energy going? Where does it want to flow? Do that and see what comes next. Then do that and see what comes next.

You can't know the plan ahead of time. It is revealed step by step in the moment. You have to trust what feels right and what you are drawn to doing and keep following that. The ego isn't comfortable with living that way, so it will try to bring you back to its plan. But just keep paying attention to the moment instead of your mind. You know you are on the right track when you feel joy. Let that be your guide.

The ego is guided by ideas, but what are ideas and where do they come from? How reliable are they, really? You are programmed to believe your ideas are true and trustworthy, but are they really? Essence is far more trustworthy. It has brought you all the joy you have ever experienced. What has the mind brought you? Mostly pain. Once you see this, the choice is really clear, but you have to be willing to see this. There is a choice to be made: Will you pay attention to your mind, or will you pay attention to what is coming out of the moment?

CHAPTER 5

THE DIVINE SPEAKS

Talking to the Divine

It is easy to talk to the Divine because you have a direct line to it. You are never apart from it. No matter how apart you may feel, the Divine is right here with you, sharing and participating in this life with you, because the Divine *is* you and everything else. It doesn't abandon its creations, but lives inside them, silently and unobtrusively. It makes itself known in every moment, but it is hidden from plain view by its subtlety and non-demanding nature, and it is overshadowed by the prominence of the egoic mind.

Because it is undetectable by your senses and incomprehensible to your mind, the Divine is not felt to be real; and yet, it created all that you consider real. It is the matrix behind all life. You can't see it or touch it, but you can and do experience it. You are never not experiencing it because you are its hands, eyes, ears, legs, and mouths in the world. It moves you through life, has experience through you, and evolves as a result of those experiences.

The Divine is more real than this *you* that you think you are, which is more like a dream that the Divine conjured. The Divine allows the dreamer to manipulate the dream, but ultimately, the Divine creates the dream and determines when it will end for the dreamer. The Divine determines the setting, the general plot, and the characters this dreamer will meet, then it allows the dreamer to respond as the dreamer will. There is free will inside this dream, although outside of it, there is only one will that chooses to have the experience of the dream, whatever that might be.

One characteristic of this dream is that the dreamer can realize it is a dream while still inside it. After that, he or she is freer to co-create with the Dream Maker. The dream goes better at this point because the dreamer makes wiser choices, has access to more resources and helpers, and has more power to influence the dream and its characters. The dreamer becomes more like a superhero in the midst of any trouble that arises in the dream because now the dreamer knows his or her true nature and no longer falls prey to fears and false ideas. The problems that arise are easily conquered because they are known to be unreal, created by one's own mind. The challenges brought by the dream are welcome and only serve to strength the dreamer.

One reason the dream goes well once the dreamer has realized that it is a dream is that the lines of communication between the dreamer and the Dream Maker are open: The dreamer can talk to the Dream Maker, and the Dream Maker talks back. Before that, the dreamer was unaware of the Dream Maker and felt alone and didn't ask for help. Help was available, but the dreamer didn't know it. The dreamer had to learn to ask for help and then listen for the answer. Once the dreamer did this, it made it possible to wake up out of the dream while still inside it.

The lines of communication between you and the Divine are always open, but until you open them on your end, you can't receive the full benefit. If you don't know that communication is possible and already happening, you are likely to miss it because you won't be listening, and you won't be taking advantage of it by asking for help. The Divine communicates to you constantly, but when you are involved with the mind, you often miss it. When your mind is quiet, you just might catch it. But if you don't believe the message is real and helpful, you may disregard it.

Recognizing that such communication is possible is a big step in your evolution. It is a real breakthrough for the Divine because it gives the Divine an opportunity to have more of an influence. Before this, the mind is expected to guide your life. After this, it is possible to see that something else is guiding your life. You will still have challenges, but they will be ones designed by the Divine for your growth, not problems your egoic mind has made up or actually created.

It is more important to listen to the Divine than to talk to it because it is always conveying something to you whether you talk to it or not. Nevertheless, talking to the Divine—especially asking questions— sets the stage for listening and can bring you specific insights you might not ordinarily catch. Talking to the Divine opens up the channel of communication and makes it more likely you will receive the insight and understanding you need to move through life more easily. You can ask for guidance on specific issues, and you will receive it. For instance, if you are trying to make a decision, you can pose a question and wait for a response, which will often come energetically, intuitively, or occasionally through words. The answer to any question may change over time, so it is important to keep checking to see if the guidance you received still holds true.

Prayer is another word for talking to the Divine. But rather than pleading to God to deliver what *you* want, you ask the Divine to reveal what *it* wants. Those are two very different approaches to the Divine. One assumes that getting what you want is the goal, regardless of what is best for the Whole; the other asks the Divine to help you play your part in the Whole. The personal self is recognized as a vehicle, or an instrument, for the Whole rather than a separate entity pitted against it. You surrender your will to the Divine's because you recognize that what seems like your will actually belongs to the false self, the ego, and can't be trusted and isn't a worthy guide.

What makes this kind of prayer powerful is the underlying assumption that you are not the ego or the mind. In affirming your allegiance to the Whole rather than to the ego, you are affirming your desire to be aligned with Essence over the ego. When you pray for that, Essence responds and becomes more obviously present and active in your life. Eventually you will come to know yourself as That. Acknowledging that you want to be aligned with Essence instead of the ego is a very important step in bringing this about.

If you pray for nothing else, pray for this, and the rest will be easy. This prayer, alone, has the power to bring you into alignment, where all the answers you need will be revealed.

Listening to the Divine

The Divine speaks in a number of ways. To hear it requires listening in some unusual ways because it rarely speaks in actual words. It speaks mostly through the intuition, which comes through the body and the mind.

When an intuition comes through the body, something is just known. You don't know how you know it; you just know it. This kind of knowing is usually accompanied by an energetic experience, somewhat like a solidness or heaviness, usually in the chest area. No thoughts preceded that knowing and none follow it, just a solid sense of certainty about an answer that arose from nowhere.

When an intuition comes through the mind, there is a similar knowing that was neither preceded nor followed by thoughts. Rather than occurring in the body, the intuition comes to you more like an idea, although one that isn't fully put into words. It is as if information was downloaded into your brain, and you just know. The intuition stands on its own, apart from the mind. Usually, you try to put this knowing into words. Intuition that comes through the mind is similar to symbols or pictures, which contain a lot of information and then must be interpreted. This is where some distortion might occur. The same is true of intuition that comes through the body: The information is as if it is condensed, and when it is reconstituted and put into words, it may become distorted.

Whether intuition comes through the body or the mind, there is a rightness, clarity and solidity about it that rings true. It makes sense. You trust it. You just know that it is the answer. You feel excited, happy, relieved, and at peace. You are no longer struggling to find a solution, but resting from all struggle to know because now you do know. It feels like a big "Ah-ha!"

The experience of knowing something with the mind is just the opposite. The egoic mind is rarely sure of a decision, and it is easily swayed and confused by various viewpoints. This is because the ego bases decisions on conflicting and sometimes contradictory information and because the ego wants contradictory things—it wants it all. With nearly every decision, the ego struggles. The egoic mind causes you to feel confused, unhappy, uncomfortable, and ill at ease. It wants a solution, but it can't find one, and that causes a lot of suffering.

Part of the problem is that there is a right time for every solution or answer, and the mind doesn't want to wait for a solution or answer to arise naturally. When the solution does arise, it arises through the intuition. Finally there is relief from the mind's struggle to find an answer! Unfortunately, sometimes the solution or answer comes too late because the mind has already made a decision just to ease its discomfort. In this way, the mind can lead you down a path that is not the best one for you.

When this happens, Essence does its best to work with that choice, and it continues to steer you toward creating a situation that will be more fitting and fulfilling. It continues to deliver messages intuitively, and it uses other means to communicate its plan. The Divine, through Essence, fortunately has many other voices besides the voice of intuition. One of those is the voice of others.

Essence within you collaborates with Essence within others to help bring about your plan and everyone else's. Essence within you inspires Essence within others to give you the messages, help, information, advice, support, comfort, love, and encouragement you need to unfold your plan. If you aren't accepting the guidance Essence offers you intuitively, it will have others voice it. Getting advice and information from others is generally more acceptable, credible, and trustworthy to the mind.

When you are not in touch with your intuition or not listening to it for whatever reason (usually your mind or someone else is telling you not to), Essence tries to get your attention by using other people to voice its guidance. It inspires others to say what you need to hear. You have had this happen countless times, and you have been a mouthpiece for

Essence countless times. It happens more than you probably imagine. You pass on and receive not only life-altering information, but also information that can make life better in small ways.

The most meaningful and fulfilling interchanges between people are ones that involve Essence. One sign this is happening is that you feel good afterward and often inspired to take some kind of action. Interchanges between egos, on the other hand, leave you confused, defensive, feeling bad, or at best unchanged.

Essence changes lives for the better because it moves people in directions that are meaningful. The ego can't do this because it doesn't know what would be meaningful for someone. And what the ego assumes would be meaningful probably would not be. The egoic mind is not in a position to be able to guide life, and yet it is what most people turn to for answers.

The Divine also speaks through events. Sometimes it creates events to make you question or change your direction. When things aren't going well, it may be that the situation is not aligned with Essence. Essence may try to convince you to surrender to its plan by not allowing you to have what you want or to continue to go in a particular direction. People suffer greatly when this happens, but once the new direction becomes established, their lives will be changed for the better.

If this seems to be happening to you, it is good to consciously surrender, that is, make a statement of surrender and ask what is wanted of you. Putting yourself in a receptive mode rather than feeling like a victim will shift your consciousness and allow you to receive the insight you need to move things in a different direction. You may have to do this repeatedly over a period of time before clarity arises.

Essence often needs time to bring you the information, people, and opportunities that will help you be open to a new direction. Without these, intuitive suggestions are likely to be rejected because they may seem too abstract and implausible. Life often has to make you aware of and get you thinking about some possibility before you will trust your intuition enough to act on it. Intuitions concerning major life changes nearly always go hand in hand with events and opportunities that also point to it.

So Essence speaks to you both by blocking certain directions and by making it possible to move gracefully in certain directions. You can recognize the direction Essence intends because you will experience the following:

1) <u>Numerous pointers</u> to it. For example, you are told about it by several people, someone gives you a book about it, you see a TV program about it, your close friend is doing it, you have a dream about it, you get excited when you think about it.

2) <u>Support and opportunities</u> to move in that direction. For example, someone offers you a job or offers to pay your schooling or train you, family members or close friends are doing it or encouraging you to do it.

3) <u>Ease</u> in moving in that direction. For example, you already have the skills for it, no other opportunities are presenting themselves, no one is discouraging you, nothing is in the way, there is no reason not to.

If the direction you are moving in is short on obvious pointers, opportunities, support, and ease, it may not be right for you at this time. This doesn't mean you should change directions whenever something is difficult. Life is difficult at times, and sometimes persistence is required to achieve Essence's goals. However, if your direction is aligned with Essence, you will have the strength, motivation, courage, inspiration, and assistance to overcome the challenges. If it is not, you will feel dispirited and not have the inspiration, motivation, and courage to continue or the assistance you need to succeed.

So whether your direction is the right one for you or not is revealed by your feelings about it: The right direction feels right no matter what difficulties are encountered. The wrong direction feels unfulfilling no matter what degree of success is encountered.

Expressions of the Divine

The Divine expresses itself in the world in ways other than just by guiding and shaping your destinies. It expresses itself, like you do, for the pure joy of it. It created this world to grow, learn, and evolve, and for the opportunities the world provides to be creative. The Divine evolves not just through work and overcoming challenges, but also through play and creativity. Creating is one of the ways the Divine grows, learns, evolves—and enjoys life.

The Divine creates primarily through you because, of all its creations on earth, humans have the most potential to be creators. Unlike other creatures, which are far more limited in their expression, you have a capacity for very diverse and complex experiences. You hold far more potential for exploration than any other life form on earth. For one thing, you have the ability to create such things as the automobile, airplane, and computer, which expand your experiences beyond what the body alone is capable of. And you have adapted to live nearly everywhere on the globe.

Each of you is a unique instrument for the Divine. No one else has ever been or will ever be exactly like you, nor will the times and circumstances you live in ever be the same. This allows for a completely unique experience through every one of you. This diversity and uniqueness is evidence for a purposefulness behind creation and, consequently, for the existence of an Intelligence behind creation, one that is also participating in creation and enjoying it.

There is no way of proving this, of course, but those of us who have evolved beyond the physical plane know this to be true. It is part of our work and service to you to explain this. Hopefully, this understanding will help you cope with the difficulties and challenges that are part of this marvelous plan.

The difficulties and challenges spur creativity on. Without them, you might not use the talents, gifts, and intellect you have been given. A Garden of Eden is really not ideal—for you or for the Divine. A world based on duality, one that has both good and evil (ignorance), offers a richer and much more interesting experience. The Divine loves a heroic story, one in which the hero is pitted against ignorance or difficult circumstances and must use his or her ingenuity, strength, and love to overcome those difficulties.

This life is all about such stories, which are also evidence for an Intelligence guiding life. The Divine guides life in a specific direction—toward greater goodness, strength, courage, compassion, tolerance, kindness, patience, wisdom, and love. Humanity is evolving in this direction, not the opposite, and that is no coincidence or accident. Love is what life is all about. Life is intended to bring you back to Love.

CONCLUSION

THE RETURN TO LOVE

Humanity is evolving, and it is evolving toward love. The evolution toward love is evidence of the Divine in the world. It is being accomplished through challenges, which teach love. It may be difficult to see how this is possible; challenges so often result in suffering and defeat. But when they don't, they reap the opposite: love, strength, compassion, wisdom, understanding, patience, and tolerance.

Over the course of your many lifetimes, you learn to turn challenges into strengths. Every challenge has a positive potential—every one. Equally, every challenge has a negative potential: It can result in fear, hatred, anger, blame, hopelessness, vengeance, ruthlessness, cruelty, or abuse. Even mildly challenging circumstances can result in terrible experiences of pain and suffering.

What makes the difference is what aspect of yourself responds to the challenges—the ego or Essence. In any one moment, one or the other steps up and reacts. What most determines what reacts is your level of evolution, but many other factors are also involved. Even older, more advanced souls might react negatively to trying situations under certain circumstances, especially initially. The ego is often the first thing to kick in whenever you or someone you love is threatened. For example, even very gentle people can become very angry at drivers whom they perceive as threatening.

However, during stressful and difficult times, particularly in emergency situations, many people also experience a strength and power moving through them that is beyond them. Even those who are very entrenched in the ego may get taken over by Essence in extreme situations when that is necessary to save someone's life. The Divine often steps in and saves life. Those who experience this describe it this way too. Most heroes don't feel they can take credit for their heroism, and that is why. The ego can't take credit for it. The Divine saves life when that life is meant to be preserved.

This is what is usually thought of as heroism. But if heroism is defined as goodness prevailing over the ego, then heroism happens countless times every day. Every time goodness (God-ness) prevails, that is Essence taking over life—that is the hero in you overcoming the challenge of the ego, slaying the dragon of untruth.

Notice how often this happens in your life and in others' lives in just one day. Notice all the times you or someone else chooses love, kindness, generosity, helpfulness, and attentiveness over selfishness and self-concern. That is Essence living through you and living through them. The Divine is everywhere in disguise as ordinary human beings of all kinds.

There isn't a human being on this planet who has less access to Essence than another. Essence is an equal opportunity employer—it is equally accessible to everyone. It may seem less accessible to some because it is buried by ego identification, but it is only less visible. The instant anyone chooses love over selfishness or self-concern, there Essence is, regardless of how evolved or spiritual that person is. You don't have to be aware of Essence or believe in it for it to be living through you. It lives through all people regardless of their beliefs because *it is who they are*. They cannot *not* express Essence. It is what moves them, and it allows the ego to step in and move them as well. Every time the ego speaks or acts, Essence is allowing it.

Essence allows you to have the experience you choose to have, for the most part. Sometimes Essence overrides the ego briefly to steer life in a particular direction, and then it steps back again and allows you to identify with the ego again, if you choose to. This dance between Essence and the ego is ongoing in everyone. Some choose to express the ego more than Essence, and some choose to express Essence more than the ego. But eventually, everyone expresses Essence more than the ego because that is the direction of evolution.

Love is the only satisfying choice, so eventually everyone chooses it over the ego. Everyone overcomes the programming that causes ego identification. Without exception, that is where everyone is headed. No matter how heinous a crime someone has committed, he or she will end up a saint in some other lifetime. The story has a happy ending. The hero slays the dragon once and for all.

The egoic programming is overcome because the suffering caused by it becomes unacceptable. Solutions to that suffering are sought, and the truth becomes known: The ego is an imposter *and* the source of all suffering. Seeing the truth frees you only somewhat from your programming because the program is still running. It can still draw you back into ego identification and suffering—and it does, even once you become strongly aligned with Essence. Evolution continues for quite a while before Essence becomes established as the state you live from most of the time.

Choosing Essence over the ego is a heroic act because it is not the easy choice. The easy choice is to follow your programming, your thoughts. It turns out that following your thoughts is not so easy, really, because ego identification is so unsatisfying and ultimately leads to unhappiness. Still, this has to be seen and a choice made to forego the temptations of the ego and "settle" for peace, love, and contentment, which are not nearly as glamorous as what the ego promises.

The ego promises riches, beauty, acclaim, success, and adoration. These are its ultimate goals, which it believes it needs to be happy. It reaches for unattainable goals that will never deliver the happiness that is promised even if they are attained, which is what people do discover. The ego tells you that you can never be happy with simply being, loving, giving, and accepting. It tells you the opposite of the truth.

To discover the truth, you have to go against that programming and the programming of others, who reinforce these lies, and that is a heroic act. Heroes are not afraid to stand up for the truth, to buck the crowd to do what feels right and good. They have the courage to make the difficult choice, which ends up being the easiest choice in the world. It is the choice that has been filling the world with love ever since the world existed. At a certain point in your evolution, it is the only choice left to you. Once you know the truth, you can't go back to living the lie. You can't go on believing that you exist apart from everything else. There is only one choice left, and that choice is love.

The only trick is that that choice has to be made again and again in each new moment. Essence happily makes this choice. Only when you are identified with the egoic mind does this choice seem difficult, and that is when it is most important to choose love. By choosing love over selfishness and self-concern even when it is hard to, you affirm your divinity and the truth that is all around you: The Divine exists right here and now in everyone, in everything. You are That.

APPENDIX

Excerpts from
EMBRACING THE NOW
by Gina Lake

AWARENESS IS WHO YOU ARE

Awareness always is. There is never a time when we are not aware. Even when we sleep and dream, we are aware we have slept and dreamt. Awareness is the one constant in life. It is even constant after life, for awareness—consciousness—continues even after the body has died, although after death, consciousness is no longer connected to the body. We are what is conscious of life and conscious of everything coming and going. When our attention is placed on consciousness rather than on the comings and goings in life, we feel at peace with whatever is coming and going.

Consciousness, or Awareness, is content with life in whatever way it's showing up. Who we really are is even content to have the experience of an ego that argues with whatever is showing up. Awareness participates in life by being aware of life, but unlike the ego, it doesn't try to control or change life. Awareness just is, and it allows whatever is to be the way it is, for the time being, since life is always changing into something else.

When we are aware of ourselves as Awareness, we have a very different sense of ourselves than when we are aware of ourselves as the ego. When who we are seems to be the ego, we have a specific definition of ourselves: "I am this, not that"; "I am male, not female"; "I am smart, not stupid"; "I am short, not tall." We fit into some categories and not others because the mind defines us in a particular way. In making such distinctions, the mind separates us from others. It makes us distinct from others. That is the egoic mind's job, and it does it very well.

The Awareness that we are, on the other hand, can't be defined. It has no gender, no physical dimensions, no this or that. It is not distinct from anything that is being observed. Although we might experience Awareness as a witness of life, because that's how the mind conceives of it, Awareness is not a witness, but more like *witnessing*. When we are first learning to separate ourselves from the mind, conceptualizing a witness who is observing the mind can be helpful, but that witness is not Awareness. The witness is just an idea that represents Awareness. To witness the mind, we need awareness, but making Awareness into a witness is making it into a thing, which it's not. Awareness is more like the experience of witnessing.

Learning to witness our own mind is the first step in becoming free of the ego and its conditioning. But to free ourselves from identification with the egoic mind takes more than just witnessing the mind. If we witness our mind and still believe it, we aren't any freer than when we were identified with it. To be free of our conditioning, we also have to see the falseness of it. Even so, there's one more very important step.

Many people are aware of their egoic mind and the falseness of it, but they still aren't free of it because they are still giving their attention to it. The experience is like watching a bad TV show, acknowledging that it's bad, but staying glued to the TV set. Until we put our attention on what is true instead of on what is false, we won't be free. We will still be experiencing our ego more than our true self.

To be free of the ego requires moving our attention away from our conditioned thoughts to the truth of who we are. It requires knowing ourselves as Awareness and seeing and responding to life as Awareness. When we know ourselves as Awareness, we experience our thoughts as only a small part of what's going on in any moment, not the main show. Awareness takes in all of life, not just what's showing up on the TV screen of our mind. True freedom comes from stepping back from the TV screen of our mind to a place where we can take in the rest of the room and what's going on in the rest of the room.

By becoming aware of what else is showing up in the moment, we can begin to really live in the moment and respond to it naturally, uncluttered by our mental commentary and the ego's desires. We are in the moment without the egoic mind influencing our experience of it. When the voice of the ego no longer dominates and colors the landscape of life, that is spiritual freedom, or liberation. That voice is experienced as one small aspect of the landscape, one other thing that comes and goes in the landscape. The ego's voice becomes impersonal, something in the landscape that has no more personal relevance than a bird's song or the temperature of the room. We still experience it, but we don't experience it as our voice, and we are no longer compelled to follow it or express it.

Once we gain some detachment from the ego's voice, it's possible to experience the Experiencer, the true self, the consciousness that is behind all life and behind our particular life. The Experiencer is in love with life, and when we let it live us, we are in love with life, and our actions and words express that love. Freedom from the ego brings a final relaxation into the true self and the possibility of being that in the world instead of the ego. What a relief!

BECOMING AWARE OF AWARENESS

Becoming aware of ourselves as Awareness is as easy as noticing we are aware. Awareness is so obvious that it's taken for granted, overlooked. Yet, when we turn our attention to what is aware, we get a glimpse of the mysteriousness of who we really are. What is it that is looking out of your eyes and taking in the world? What is looking isn't your eyes. Our eyes are an instrument of awareness, but awareness isn't located inside our head or body, although it seems to be. It's more like awareness is funneled through the body-mind.

At death, awareness is withdrawn, and only the body remains. Then it becomes obvious that whomever or whatever was alive was not the body. Without the animation of the body that consciousness, or the soul, brings to it, the body is just a mass of cells, inert material. When something is said to be soulless, we all know what that means. The soul, although not acknowledged by science, is evident to many who have been with someone as he or she has died.

When the soul incarnates and consciousness, or Awareness, comes into the body, the body becomes capable of being a vehicle for who we really are. The capacity to be aware is Spirit as it lives through what we call our body. We aren't actually our body, but the awareness that's operating through it, although we mistake ourselves for the body and for all the other labels given to the body and the personality.

The process of human evolution is a process of disidentification with the body, mind, and personality and a reidentification with, or a realization of, our true nature. That realization and shift in identification is called *awakening*.

Awakening is the destiny of every human being. Awakening begins by becoming aware of Awareness, by noticing and therefore experiencing more fully what's actually alive in your body. What gives your body life? That's who you really are. You are what brings life into the body and sustains it through breathing and enlivening every system. When the consciousness that you are decides to leave, the body stops being alive.

Who we are is the consciousness that allows the body to be alive and aware. The more we notice Awareness, the stronger the energetic experience that accompanies it becomes. That energetic experience is an experience of aliveness. So although who we really are isn't physical, it can be sensed physically, and it is sensed as energy, a vibrating aliveness. The energetic sense of aliveness is as close as we can get to experiencing who we really are physically. Becoming more aware of that subtle vibration, or aliveness, helps us align with our true nature.

ALIVENESS

When we are in our body and senses and not in our head, we experience a sense of aliveness that is felt as a subtle energetic vibration, or tingling, and a sense of being alive, illumined, and aware. These sensations are how who we really are is experienced by the body-mind. That aliveness is the felt-sense of who we really are and what we experience when we are in the Now. When we are aligned with who we really are and not identified with the ego, we feel that aliveness, Presence, energetically, and it's very pleasurable.

The fact that who we really are, Essence, can be felt energetically is very handy because it makes identifying when we are aligned with Essence and when we aren't easier. That sense of aliveness can also help us realign with Essence when we are identified with the ego. If you find yourself contracted and suffering, you can search for the sense of aliveness, which is always present, and focus on it. No matter how faint the experience of aliveness is, it will increase as you pay attention to it. Focusing on aliveness is a way of accessing Essence in every moment.

The more you pay attention to the aliveness, the more obvious it becomes. It can become very strong, and when it does, it acts like an anchor, grounding us in the Now and helping us stay there. The sense of aliveness can drown out the ego's mind-chatter, relegating it to the background. If we focus on the aliveness often enough as we go about our day, it will become the foreground, and the mind-chatter will fall into the background.

When we are grounded in aliveness, we experience a deep calm and peacefulness, which allows us to move through our day with equanimity. That peacefulness is unflappable, unless our emotional body gets triggered by a belief or by someone else's belief we've identified with. When that happens, the aliveness is still present and can bring us back into the Now if we give our attention to it instead of to the thoughts and feelings that were triggered.

Not buying into our thoughts and feelings doesn't make us less human, as some might think. It's just a different way of being in the world, although not the most common one. Being aligned with aliveness instead of our thoughts and feelings actually makes us more effective and functional—and also more kind—than being identified with our thoughts and feelings.

Being aligned with Essence instead of the egoic mind is the next step in humanity's evolution. Eventually we will all awaken out of the egoic mind and live from Essence. Emotions will still exist in potential, but they won't run roughshod over the body-mind. Equanimity, acceptance, and love will be the most common state instead of discontentment, striving, contraction, and fear. Certain individuals are heralding this shift in consciousness and helping to bring it about. The potential to live from Essence exists in everyone, but only some people will make that a priority. The more people who do, the easier it will be for the rest of humanity to make that shift in consciousness.

You are probably motivated to make the shift to living from Essence. Paying attention to the feeling of aliveness is one of the most useful tools for awakening. Of course, the egoic self isn't the one who chooses to do that. What chooses to give attention to the aliveness is Essence, as it awakens you. The ego will fight that choice all the way. Essence is the awareness of the whole drama between the ego and the *you* that is awakening.

NOTICING AS A DOORWAY INTO THE NOW

The present moment, the Now, is where we meet our true self. Who we really are isn't who we *think* we are. Who we really are has nothing to do with thinking and everything to do with not thinking. When we aren't involved with the egoic mind, we move into the Now and the experience of who we really are.

The ego, the sense of *me*, disappears as soon as it encounters the Now, so the ego runs from the Now. It can't survive in the Now. It's revived and survives through thought, particularly through thoughts about the past and future, but also about the present. The ego tells stories about the past, present, and future. Paying attention to these stories takes us out of the Now and into the egoic mind's made-up reality. When we are identified with the egoic mind, we live in the ego's interpretation of reality, not in reality. We live in its explanations about what is, what was, and what will be. These stories take us away from the living reality of the Now.

To experience the Now, we merely have to notice what's happening in the present moment without our interpretations, opinions, judgments, beliefs, or concepts. This may sound difficult, but all it takes is a shift from being absorbed in our thoughts to *noticing* our thoughts. Noticing whatever else is present in addition to our thoughts without interpreting it, judging it, or telling a story about it brings us into the Now and can keep us there as long as we continue to notice without interpreting or telling stories about what we're noticing. However, once any judgment, opinion, or belief is considered instead of just noticed, we are back in the mind and identified with the ego again instead of with Essence.

Whenever we notice and become fully involved in what *is* without becoming involved in any mental activity, Essence becomes apparent. Noticing is a doorway to experiencing Essence because noticing is a quality of who we really are. Essence is often referred to as Awareness because who we are is the Awaring Presence that is conscious and aware of everything. Essence is joyously participating in its creation by being aware of what it has created, including itself manifesting as an individual.

When we stop and ask, "Who am I?" what we find is nothing. We find only Presence, Awareness, Consciousness, which is aware of the thoughts, feelings, sensations, and experiences of the individual that we assume we are. This Awareness, this noticing of everything, is who we really are! When we realize we are Awareness—the Noticer— then it makes sense that noticing is a way back to Essence.

Once we have realized Essence through noticing, then allowing is necessary in order to stay in contact with Essence. Our noticing must be infused with allowing and without any mental activity. Or if there is mental activity, then that's noticed. The ego, on the other hand, does the opposite of allowing. When it notices something, it labels it, judges it, and relates it back to how it will affect *me*. As soon as we become engaged with the mind, allowing stops and resistance takes its place. We become identified, once again, with the *me*, the false self that opposes life, rather than with who we really are.

The Awareness that is our true nature is aware of everything that may be part of any moment: thoughts, feelings, desires, sensations, energy, sights, sounds, inner experiences, intuitions, urges, inspirations, and much more. When we are noticing and allowing, we also are aware of these things. As a result of being aware, a knowing might arise about an action to take. Activity naturally arises from being aware of what *is* in each moment.

The ego has its own experience of each moment and attends to only a small portion of what can be experienced in any moment. The ego acts in keeping with its limited perceptions and sense of separateness. These actions are often very different from the actions Essence would take.

Essence allows us to follow the ideas and feelings generated by the ego if doing so doesn't interfere with Essence's intentions, because part of what Essence intends is that we explore the world and create according to our ideas and feelings. Essence is interested in seeing what we will create, but it also has intentions of its own and many ways of guiding us toward them. It also participates in creation by inspiring spontaneous action—action that arises without prior thought.

So you could say there are two types of activity: activity instigated by the ego and activity inspired by Essence. Both are often going on simultaneously. As we evolve, Essence begins to live through us more, and ego-driven activity structures our life less.

Noticing is an important spiritual practice for getting in touch with Essence and with how it's moving us. Essence is very active in our lives and can be more active the more we acknowledge it as a motivating force. The less attention we give the egoic mind and its suggestions for how to live, and the more attention (notice) we give Essence and its drives and inspiration, the more smoothly and happily we move through life. Noticing and allowing are key spiritual practices that align us with our true nature and support Essence's intentions for us.

AWARENESS MEDITATION

Meditation is such an important practice because it acquaints us with Essence and trains us to move out of our mind. The state of ego identification is reinforced whenever we believe the egoic mind and the feelings it generates. When we buy into the ego's perceptions, the ego is strengthened. To discover that other perceptions and another way of life exist, we have to turn away from the mind, which has been so empowered by the attention we have given it.

Breaking the pattern of paying attention to the egoic mind takes commitment, and the ego will fight us every step of the way. It resists by balking at meditation, telling us that meditation won't help or isn't helping, that it's too hard, that we don't like it, or that we don't have time. The ego digs up excuses for not meditating.

When we do meditate, the ego chats incessantly at us. It also stirs up fears about what we might experience during meditation and how that might change our life. The dissolution of the ego that happens in meditation can feel frightening, but that fear is natural. Fear is what the ego uses, and always has used, to control us. The ego is only open to meditation because of the possibility of having a spiritual experience that would feel good and make it feel special. If special experiences aren't happening, the ego won't stay interested in meditation.

There's no good reason not to meditate and every reason to meditate. Meditation is the most important thing you can do to support awakening. For most people, a practice of meditation or something similar is necessary to awaken and embody that awakeness in daily life.

Meditating doesn't have to be complicated. It's as simple as anything can be. What's difficult about meditating is committing time to it daily. The regularity of meditation is important in order to counteract the reinforcement we are habitually giving the egoic mind by being so involved with it.

Something else very important happens when we commit ourselves to a practice of meditation: Spiritual forces that are assisting our evolution are summoned. Affirming our desire to awaken and backing it up with a practice of meditation sends a clear signal to nonphysical forces that we are ready to awaken, and they take it as a cue to help us wake up.

Meditation is as simple as just sitting and noticing, or being aware of, what's occurring—what's coming into our senses; what energetic sensations are being experienced; what thoughts, feelings intuitions, inspirations, drives, and urges are arising— without getting involved in the mind's commentary about these things. Getting us involved in its commentary is how the egoic mind takes us out of the Now. If we follow its train of thought, we will no longer experience the fullness of the Now, but only a small slice of it.

The goal of meditation is to experience our true nature, or Essence. Essence is the noticing, aware Presence that we imitate when we sit down to meditate. In imitating Awareness by being aware of everything we are experiencing in the moment (but not identifying with it), we *become* that Awareness, we drop into it. Noticing without getting involved in any thoughts about what we are noticing aligns us with Essence.

When we are aligned with Essence, our experience of the moment changes. Our boundaries soften, we may feel a sense of expansion, and the sense of *me* falls into the background or disappears altogether. Peace, contentment, acceptance, gratitude, compassion, love, and any number of other positive qualities may arise. These qualities are indications of Essence. When we give our attention to those qualities, the experience of them increases.

It's possible to achieve quite a blissful state by meditating, although that isn't the goal. The goal isn't to achieve a particular good feeling, but to experience Essence and what it intends. Essence is here, living through us. It is incarnate, and it intends to have certain experiences and accomplish certain things through us. It doesn't push us like the ego, but inspires us through joy to involve ourselves in certain activities. In meditation, we feel Essence's joy in being alive through us, and we may receive guidance from Essence intuitively.

We find peace and contentment in meditating and a welcome respite from the ego's world of striving. We also find true motivation. Meditation brings us into the Now, where we can discover how Essence is moving us. When the mind is out of the way, Essence can guide us more easily. Meditation is far from an escape from life, which is what the ego thinks. Instead, it allows us to align more truly with the life we were meant to live.

THE SIMPLEST MEDITATION

Here's the simplest meditation, which you can do anywhere and anytime. It's meant to become a way of life, not just a meditation: Notice, without getting involved in any thoughts about what you are noticing. Ignore all of the mind's commentary. Notice not only what's obvious, such as what you are seeing, but also what's more subtle, such as your inner experience and state, your energy and sense of yourself (is it expanded or contracted?), any knowing or intuitions, any drives or motivations, and any thoughts or feelings. Notice not only what's coming in through your senses, but also the impact that has on you subtly and not so subtly. Notice everything that's arising in the moment and being experienced. And if you are involved in doing something, really notice that. There's a lot to notice in any moment!

The reason for meditating is to develop your ability to stay present to thoughts and feelings, which are products of the ego, instead of identify with them. We habitually identify with the egoic mind—we believe our thoughts and feelings—and this causes a lot of suffering. The ego isn't wise, and it keeps us from accessing true guidance and from recognizing what is really living our life. Through noticing, awareness of the Noticer is strengthened. Another name for the Noticer is Essence. The Noticer is who we really are. We are what is noticing, or aware of, life.

This simple meditation helps us get in touch with what we are actually always doing: noticing. However, when we are identified with thoughts and feelings, we lose awareness of the Noticer, which is still there, of course. Getting to know ourselves as the Noticer instead of the egoic mind is what spiritual practices and meditation in particular are all about. Spiritual practices are meant to bring us an experience of Essence. What we are isn't something in another dimension or apart from us; it's right here, noticing the letters on this page. Who do you think is reading this? That which is alive and conscious is reading this, and that is who you really are. Who you really are isn't hidden and apart from life, but engaged and embodied in it.

We are programmed with a sense of being a *me*, with certain desires, thoughts, and ways of being in the world. But who we really are is what is able to notice our desires, thoughts, and tendencies. We are programmed to think we are the *me*, but we are actually what's aware of and able to contemplate the *me*. Moreover, we are what can choose to do what the *me* wants or not. Once we're no longer identified with the *me*, we can choose how the *me* will express itself in the world. The *me* doesn't have to be run by the ego, which tends to make negative and selfish choices.

Once Essence takes over, and your choices come from it rather than from the ego, life goes much better. The simple act of noticing is one of the most powerful things you can do to transform your life because noticing moves you out of ego identification and into Essence.

MEDITATING ON WHAT IS

Meditation is the practice of keeping our attention focused on something that's coming in through our senses: the air moving in and out as you breathe; the movement of energy in your body; a mantra, music, or other sounds; a candle flame, a mandala, something beautiful, or a guru's picture. The practice is to bring your attention back to these sensory experiences whenever you find yourself caught up in a thought. When you notice you are thinking, gently bring your attention back to whatever you are focusing on.

The purpose of this practice is not only to feel peace, but to train ourselves to be more permanently in our senses and in the experience of the moment rather than in the mind and its version of reality. For most people, meditation provides temporary relief and respite from life and from the mind. However, with a regular and dedicated practice of meditation (an hour or more a day), the effects of meditation spill over into everyday life and influence how we experience life and how we are in life. That's wonderful news and a very good reason to meditate.

Nevertheless, meditation can be much more than something we practice once or twice a day. Every moment can be a meditation by learning to be present to whatever we're doing or whatever is going on. Being present is a matter of attending to our sensory experience and not becoming involved in the mind's commentary about that or about something else. As with meditation, being present to life is a matter of getting fully involved in whatever you are experiencing and bringing yourself back to that experience whenever you get caught up in a thought.

Functional thought has a place in our day, of course. We need our minds to read, calculate, study, plan, write, drive, design, and do all the other things we do in our busy lives. The thoughts we don't need, and the ones that meditation and being present train us to ignore, are the ones about *me* and how it's going for the *me*. These thoughts belong to the egoic mind (the ego-driven, or chatterbox, mind), not to the functional mind. The egoic mind, which takes us out of the Now with evaluations, judgments, stories, fears, doubts, and ideas about the past and future, is not functional, but dysfunctional. It draws us out of the *experience* of life and into its story about life, which is a place of dryness, contraction, discontentment, and unhappiness. The ego is an unhappy and negative self. Fortunately, it isn't who we really are.

Learning to be present to what *is* and stay present to that takes a lot of practice. All of our lives we've been practicing giving our attention to the egoic mind, so some effort is needed to neutralize this habit. Detaching from the mind isn't easy and requires a lot of diligence, but the alternative is quite unpleasant! People often don't realize there is an alternative to listening to the chatterbox mind, but there is: Something else is living life, and the egoic mind just chatters away, pretending it's the one in control. The ego isn't who we really are, although it pretends to be, and it isn't in control, although Essence allows us to follow the egoic mind if we choose.

The more accustomed to being present we become, the more we begin to live as Essence. The Now is not only a place of sensory experience, although that is sufficiently rich, but also where life comes out of. If we aren't paying attention to the Now, we might miss what life is trying to bring about through us. We can follow the egoic mind's plans and ideas for our life if we want to, but something else right here and now has a plan, and that plan will be much more satisfying than anything the ego has to offer.

ALIGNING WITH ESSENCE

We are actually already aligned with Essence because we are Essence! We can't be anything other than Essence, but we are under the illusion that we are the roles we play and the ideas we have about ourselves. The *I* that we think of ourselves as is just the idea *I*. Like every other concept, the *I* has no objective reality. The idea *I* gives us a sense of existing separately from others and from the rest of life, but the *I* is just the thought *I*. Sit with this revelation a moment. Your sense of self is derived from a set of ideas about yourself, which came from others and from conclusions you drew about yourself because of your experiences.

The *I* is so adorned with images, beliefs, opinions, desires, fears, and feelings that it can be difficult to see that these, too, are just ideas, or stem from ideas. We have quite a complete image of ourselves in our mind, and people reinforce each other's self-images. The experience of our body as a boundary between ourselves and other people completes the picture of who we think we are. We believe we exist within the limits of our body. It does seem that way, but we don't actually exist within that boundary or in any particular location. Rather our soul, or spirit, gets assigned to a body-mind, and we take that body-mind as who we are.

Aligning with Essence is a matter of realizing that we are not the body-mind we are functioning through but the essence of life itself, poured into, if you will, a particular body-mind. The essence of life that we are doesn't fit inside one body-mind, so our body-mind is hardly a complete representation of who we really are. We are squeezed into this container, which shapes and limits our expression. The container is that of a human being (at least this time around!). We are just playing at being a human being, and we have played at being a human being in many other lifetimes. We are learning certain lessons that belong to this particular life form, and we will go on to experience other forms, including nonphysical ones.

The mind isn't designed to comprehend the truth about who we really are, nor is it designed to believe the truth. Nevertheless, a part of us does know the truth and resonates with the sense of being much vaster than we seem to be. That larger sense of ourselves is what calls us Home.

The experience of our true nature is always available, since Essence has never been anything but here all along. To be aligned with Essence, there's nowhere we have to get to. Aligning with Essence isn't something we do but happens more as a result of allowing and noticing what we already are and suspending our belief that we are who we *think* we are.

When our thoughts stop or aren't given attention, Essence shines through. Thoughts temporarily obscure, or cloud, the experience of Essence, but Essence is always there, aware of the character it's playing and all the thoughts that character is having. Essence is aware of the beliefs, opinions, fears, dreams, feelings, desires, and judgments of this character, and Essence allows it to have these thoughts and do what it will do with them. When the actor begins to wake up out of the role that he or she has been playing and glimpses the truth, the truth propels him or her on the spiritual path.

Aligning with Essence is a matter of turning our attention in every moment to our true nature rather than to the illusory false self. We wake up out of the dream of the false self into the reality of our true nature. What a dream it has been!

GOING DEEPER INTO ESSENCE

Being in our senses brings us into the Now. When we really take in what we are seeing, hearing, feeling, and tasting without becoming involved in our mind's commentary about it, we are in the Now. But there's much more to being in the Now than sensory experience. Our senses are only a doorway into the Now. The joy of being in the Now goes beyond the pleasure of the senses. To go deeper into Essence, there's another very important step, once we are fully sensing without the interference of the mind's commentary, and that is to fully experience the *effect* that sensory experience has on our Being.

When you look at a beautiful flower or hear a bird sing, what impact does that have on your internal, energetic experience? What is your Being experiencing? What is Essence's experience of that? Just take a moment and discover what Essence is experiencing for yourself. Look at something beautiful. Really take it in and notice how beauty makes you feel, not emotionally, but energetically within your being.

When we really take in beauty or anything else we are experiencing through our senses, we feel our Being celebrating and rejoicing in the moment, and we experience that energetically. That subtle energetic experience is the experience of the Heart, or Essence. That subtle joy, expansion, relaxation, yes to life is the radical happiness that comes from experiencing life as Essence experiences it.

That subtle experiencing is ongoing and ever-present, but we often don't notice our Being celebrating life because thinking is more obvious and compelling, even though thinking is actually less rewarding. Because thinking is our default position as humans, we have to *learn* to notice what else is present besides thoughts. We have to learn to notice what's real and true. We have to train ourselves to pay attention to the subtle joy, expansion, relaxation and yes of Essence as it enjoys life through us. That subtle experience becomes less subtle and easier to notice the more we put our attention on it rather than on our thoughts. Then the mind becomes quieter, softer, and more in the background.

Since the egoic mind is the generator of all suffering, it's really good to know that it doesn't have to be prominent and that something else that's much truer and more pleasant can take its place. Our Being, Essence, is happy in every moment. Just notice that. Notice how your Heart expands when you see beauty, hear a sound, or simply experience what's arising in the moment in some other way. Notice how much you actually love life. Your love for life is always accessible just by noticing it.

ABOUT THE AUTHOR

Gina Lake is a spiritual teacher and the author of numerous books about awakening to one's true nature, including *Trusting Life, Embracing the Now, Radical Happiness, Living in the Now, Return to Essence, Loving in the Moment, What About Now? Anatomy of Desire,* and *Getting Free.* She is also a gifted intuitive with a master's degree in counseling psychology and over twenty years experience supporting people in their spiritual growth. Her website offers information about her books, free e-books, book excerpts, a monthly newsletter, a blog, and audio and video recordings:

www.radicalhappiness.com

Books by Gina Lake

(Available in paperback, Kindle, and other e-book formats.)

Trusting Life: Overcoming the Fear and Beliefs That Block Peace and Happiness. Fear and distrust keep us from living the life we were meant to live, and they are the greatest hurdles to seeing the truth about life—that it is good, abundant, supportive, and potentially joyous. *Trusting Life* is a deep exploration into the mystery of who we are, why we suffer, why we don't trust life, and how to become more trusting. It offers evidence that life is trustworthy and tools for overcoming the fear and beliefs that keep us from falling in love with life.

Loving in the Moment: Moving from Ego to Essence in Relationships. Having a truly meaningful relationship requires choosing love over your conditioning, that is, your ideas, fantasies, desires, images, and beliefs. *Loving in the Moment* describes how to move beyond conditioning, judgment, anger, romantic illusions, and differences to the experience of love and Oneness with another. It explains how to drop into the core of your Being, where Oneness and love exist, and be with others from there.

Embracing the Now: Finding Peace and Happiness in What Is. The Now—this moment—is the true source of happiness and peace and the key to living a fulfilled and meaningful life. *Embracing the Now* is a collection of essays that can serve as daily reminders of the deepest truths. Full of clear insight and wisdom, it explains how the mind keeps us from being in the moment, how to move into the Now and stay there, and what living from the Now is like. It also explains how to overcome stumbling blocks to being in the Now, such as fears, doubts, misunderstandings, judgments, distrust of life, desires, and other conditioned ideas that are behind human suffering.

Radical Happiness: A Guide to Awakening provides the keys to experiencing the happiness that is ever-present and not dependent on circumstances. This happiness doesn't come from getting what you want, but from wanting what is here now. It comes from realizing that who you think you are is not who you really are. This is a radical perspective! *Radical Happiness* describes the nature of the egoic state of consciousness and how it interferes with happiness, what awakening and enlightenment are, and how to live in the world after awakening.

Living in the Now: How to Live as the Spiritual Being That You Are. The 99 essays in *Living in the Now* will help you realize your true nature and live as that. They answer many question raised by the spiritual search and offer wisdom on subjects such as fear, anger, happiness, aging, boredom, desire, patience, faith, forgiveness, acceptance, love, commitment, hope, purpose, meaning, meditation, being present, emotions, trusting life, trusting your Heart, and many other deep subjects. These essays will help you become more conscious, present, happy, loving, grateful, at peace, and fulfilled. Each essay stands on its own and can be used for daily contemplation.

Anatomy of Desire: How to Be Happy Even When You Don't Get What You Want will help you discriminate between your Heart's desires and the ego's and to relate to the ego's desires in a way that reduces suffering and increases joy. By pointing out the myths about desire that keep us tied to our ego's desires and the suffering they cause, *Anatomy of Desire* will help you be happy regardless of your desires and whether you are attaining them. So it is also about spiritual freedom, or liberation, which comes from following the Heart, our deepest desires, instead of the ego's desires. It is about becoming a lover of life rather than a desirer.

Return to Essence: How to Be in the Flow and Fulfill Your Life's Purpose describes how to get into the flow and stay there and how to live life from there. Being in the flow and not being in the flow are two very different states. One is dominated by the ego-driven mind, which is the cause of suffering, while the other is the domain of Essence, the Divine within each of us. You are meant to live in the flow. The flow is the experience of Essence—your true self—as it lives life through you and fulfills its purpose for this life.

Getting Free: How to Move Beyond Conditioning and Be Happy. Freedom from your conditioning is possible, but the mind is a formidable opponent to freedom. To be free requires a new way of thinking or, rather, not thinking. To a large extent, healing our conditioning involves changing our relationship to our mind and discovering who we really are. *Getting Free* will help you do that. It will also help you reprogram your mind; clear negative thoughts and self-images; use meditation, prayer, forgiveness, and gratitude; work with spiritual forces to assist healing and clear negativity; and heal entrenched issues from the past.

What About Now? Reminders for Being in the Moment. The secret to happiness is moving out of the mind and learning to delight in each moment. In *What About Now*, you will find over 150 quotes from Gina Lake's books—*Radical Happiness, Embracing the Now, Loving in the Moment, Living in the Now*, and others—that will inspire and enable you to be more present. These empowering quotes will wake you up out of your ordinary consciousness and help you live with more love, contentment, gratitude, and awe.

For more info, please visit the "Books" page:

www.radicalhappiness.com

Made in the USA
Lexington, KY
30 April 2012